Christmas to Calvary

Life and Memories of Jesus

by
Anthony T. Padovano

Paulist Press/New York/Mahwah

Photo credits

page 6, courtesy of Lawrence Boadt, C.S.P.
page 18, courtesy of Lawrence Boadt, C.S.P.
page 27, courtesy of Lawrence Boadt, C.S.P.
page 44, courtesy of Lawrence Boadt, C.S.P.
page 49, courtesy of Israel Information Services, N.Y.
page 67, courtesy of Lawrence Boadt, C.S.P.
page 74, courtesy of Lawrence Boadt, C.S.P.
page 85, courtesy of Israel Information Services, N.Y.

Cover photo ©1987 by
Richard Nowitz

Library of Congress Cataloging-in-Publication Data

Padovano, Anthony T.
    Christmas to Calvary.

    1. Jesus Christ—Passion—Meditations.   2. Jesus
Christ—Crucifixion—Meditations.   I. Title.
BT431.P24   1987   232.9′01   87-13406
ISBN 0-8091-2907-8 (pbk.)

Published by Paulist Press
997 Macarthur Boulevard
Mahwah, New Jersey 07430

Printed and bound in the
United States of America

Contents

	Preface	1
I	Vigil	5
II	Passover	17
III	A Paschal Homily	43
IV	Gethsemane to Grave	47
V	A Eulogy at the Tomb	66
VI	Advent Watch	71
VII	Sunday Sunrise	83

*For my
brother priests*

Preface

In other lives, we behold our own. Biography at its best is autobiography in some way.

Some lives are more significant than others. We do not say that these lives are more worthy, more important or more meaningful. They are, as we have said, more "significant." The word "significant" implies that they have a more impressive "sign" value; they are richly endowed with symbolism and metaphor so that other lives are interpreted or clarified through them.

The role we are destined to play for one another is not only a role of immediate love and service. In some way, each of us is a mirror or a sign through which others discover or encounter who they are. A few lives reach levels of such significance that the memory of them is preserved carefully lest something about all of us be lost.

In the presence of a significant life, we behold not only our own life as it is but possibilities and potential for the future. A significant life first reflects and then shapes us. At the proper level of influence we become the person we emulate even as we remain decisively the unique person we are meant to be.

It is possible that the life of Jesus may be the most "significant" life ever lived. There are elements in that life that only memory can retrieve. The memory we have of any life is not only a record of what that life was like in itself but a record of how that life impacted on our own. The memory of others is the memory of ourselves.

The events commemorated from Thursday to Easter Sunday recall the significance of the life of Jesus and celebrate that significance. There is no time in the Christian calendar when memory is richer, when celebration is more intense, when the juxtaposition of tragedy and joy is so immediate. The collective memory of the Christian family reaches over millennia and centers not only on the life of Jesus but on themes in that life that go back to the dawn of human history. On such days more than a billion people are summoned to memory and celebration. The project of human social justice may be more influenced by these contemplative memories and liturgical celebrations than by all the concrete plans for reform and equity formulated throughout our lifetime.

The events which begin at Christmas terminate on Calvary where both cross and tomb, crucifixion and new life occur. These reflections will center on the final episodes in the life of Jesus but they will be tied to the origins and maturity of his preceding life which give them meaning. The title of the book, *Christmas to Calvary,* intends not the cross as the last event in the life of Jesus but Easter, as the final act in the drama. Calvary is not only where the death occurs but the place where the tomb is found empty.

This book will contain four conference meditations and three homilies. The purpose of these materials is assistance for those who do pastoral ministry in the Church and devotional resource for those who are drawn to the life of Jesus by discipleship and desire.

The life of Jesus occasions universal human celebration. As Jesus is recalled it becomes more difficult to exclude others and to treat them insensitively. As Jesus is celebrated, we find that we celebrate not only him but also ourselves. In Christ, one participates in a cosmic dance, in the music of the spheres, in the universal cycle of life and death and life again. This is a circle that has no end, a ring of life that embraces everyone. This biography is our autobiography.

I

Vigil

Life has a way of justifying most of our hopes. We often receive the realities we ardently await. Vigil is a substantive part of the real world we inhabit. The greatest surprises and joys are not as unexpected as we imagine. At some level they are expected, longed for, yearned after, desired.

Life also has a way of fulfilling our fears. Tragedy is feared long before it arrives. It is sometimes sought, consciously or otherwise.

And, so, Christmas is as much a set of choices and vigils as it is an event of destiny and miracle.

These days of reflection are a privileged time. We are on sacred ground. We shall take off our shoes during these days and our feet will be washed. We shall drink wine and break bread. We shall pray in the darkness and dance in the light. We shall suffer together in the inner recesses of our hearts. We shall recognize our sins and feel redemption. We shall mark the sun set on Good Friday and be together as the sun rises on Easter Sunday morning. We shall become a community as our vigils and our hopes intermingle, as grief passes into glory, tragedy into triumph, loss into life. We shall stand at the man-

ger and kneel at the cross. We shall run to the tomb and find it empty and our hearts will be full.

In this first reflection, we shall consider the birth and childhood of Jesus. Matthew will be our guide. In the Holy Thursday meditation, we shall focus on Jesus, the preacher of parables. We shall take five passages from Luke which sum up the life of this young man. On Thursday, the wine will be drained, death will be in the air and the Passover joy will be muted by the imminence and finality of the passion.

On Friday, we shall remember that never before had there been such a birth or such a death. The star of his birth will be extinguished in the noonday darkness of Calvary. We shall still feel the spring air but no flowers will be visible and all the color and promise of the rainbow will be gone.

On Saturday, we shall experience a day in which everything is dead except hope. It is a vigil day of uncommon dimensions. We affirm hope where death happened. The tomb is in the garden where the spring air and the morning sun give us back the flowers and the rainbow. The star returns and a son is given to us. The manger is not empty, only the tomb. Again, on Easter, we are at table and we know Christ again in the breaking and in the wholeness. Christ fills the cup once more and we drink the fullness because we have known the absence. The passion which began as Passover is now parable.

Women play a special role in the life of Jesus. At the manger, near the cross, by the empty tomb women are the central figures in his life. On Thursday, women are not mentioned. Thursday is a day of discourse and symbol. But Christmas, Calvary, and Easter are flesh and blood events, so to speak. And women dominate.

Women figure largely in parables, miracles and discipleship, more largely than most imagine.

Matthew celebrates for us a central figure and a title for Jesus in each of the three sections of the genealogy which begins his Gospel. In the first section, Abraham is cited and Jesus is referred to as a son of Abraham so that the Jewishness of Jesus may not be called into question. Moses is not mentioned in the genealogy but Jesus will be presented as the new Moses in Matthew's Gospel. Even the infant Jesus will re-enact the life of Moses. In Matthew's Gospel alone, he will be portrayed as the sole significant survivor of a decision by a king to kill Jewish infants. This circumstance links the infant Moses and the infant Jesus. In Matthew's Gospel alone, he will come out of Egypt to the promised land. On the cross, Jesus will be condemned as King of the *Jews*. And so the Jewish credentials are clear.

In the second section, David, the prototype for kingship, is mentioned first. Jesus is, therefore, son of David. Later in the chapter, Joseph will be addressed by such a title so that Jesus will be worthy, in Matthew's account, of kingship. He is born in Bethlehem, the birthplace of David; he dies in Jerusalem, David's city; and he is condemned as *King* of the Jews.

In the third section, Jesus is the last citation. It is not only the parentage of Jesus but his title as Christ or Messiah which is made the final word of the genealogy.

The genealogy gives us all the major connections with Jewish history. This Jesus will be Jewish, royal, messianic.

There is more. The second chapter of Matthew describes a group of Gentiles, the wise men, who are moved by signs of Jesus' greatness in the heavens. They are led by light, seeing his star, as they describe it, eager to give him homage. The uni-

8

versal significance of Jesus is suggested here. Later, at the trial, Jesus will answer the question of the high priest about whether he is Son of God by alluding to heavenly phenomena. He will be seen in the future coming on the clouds of heaven.

At the cross, connections are made with the Christmas story. Once again we have a group of Gentiles, "the centurion together with the others guarding Jesus," who are moved by signs in the heavens of Jesus' greatness. They are led not by light but by darkness, the darkness over the earth from the sixth to the ninth hour. They are terrified by the earthquake and confess that the condemned man is a Son of God.

Matthew alone describes the slaughter of the innocents in the Christmas story. The angel of the Lord leads Jesus and his parents to safety. On the cross, we have the slaughter of the innocent. An angel of the Lord announces the safety of Jesus and his new family of believers. Now, it is not wise men who have seen the star but women who have seen the light of Easter. Matthew describes the Easter scene. No other evangelist describes the opening of the tomb just as no other evangelist mentions the star. The Easter scene is depicted in light. Even darkness revealed that Jesus was Son of God. But now it is light which serves as the more fitting symbol. In this regard, Easter is Christmas.

The Easter scene begins with an earthquake as the death scene had ended with an earthquake. An angel of lightning with a robe as white as snow unseals the tomb. Just as Gentile magi in the Christmas story declare Jesus King of the Jews in the city of Jerusalem, so the Gentile guards (described only in Matthew) announce the resurrection in the city of Jerusalem. Their motives are different but their description of the cosmic phenomena which accompany key events in the life of Jesus makes the point.

The wise men find Jesus in Bethlehem, the birthplace of David. The women find the risen Christ in Jerusalem, the city of David. The other disciples, the apostles, see Jesus only in Galilee, not in Jerusalem.

Women play an unusual role in the pre-history of Jesus, in the genealogy Matthew constructs. There are four women: Tamar, Rahab, Ruth and Bathsheba. The women are Gentiles or closely associated with them. Their relationship to the men in their lives is irregular, even scandalous. Tamar pretends to be a prostitute and Rahab is one. Ruth and Bathsheba are ultimately involved with their future husbands before marriage. The women, nonetheless, contribute significantly to salvation history, to the ongoing life system that eventually leads to Jesus. The point may well be that God emerges in human history in unexpected ways. Jesus, who comes from such ancestry, will forgive prostitutes as a sign of his love; he will number former prostitutes among his disciples and observe that the prostitutes enter salvation before the self-righteous. The mother of this Jesus will be suspected of having lived intimately with her future husband before marriage. The Messiah will come unexpectedly, from a mother who is presented as a virgin and a father who is a carpenter; the Messiah will come from Galilee and speak favorably of Samaritans; the Messiah will perform miracles for the Gentile Romans and reform Israel's expectations with parables for the Jewish people. Women play an unusual role in the pre-history of Jesus and in his public ministry. The women seem to be beyond the law; Jesus will be perceived in the same light.

And so Jesus is born. There are different ways to reflect on the birth. Let us deal with the birth in relationship to the prior history of Israel but more especially in relationship to the future events in the life of Jesus. The birth of Jesus is not recorded by Matthew as an event in its own right but as a relational reality. It is a theological statement on the identity of this person rather than a chronological reference point in a biography of him.

There are a number of intriguing anomalies in the infancy narratives. Matthew and Luke tell us of the birth but Mark does not; John does not; Paul does not. Even Matthew and Luke seem unaware that they have written of the infancy and the extraordinary phenomena surrounding it after the first two chapters of their respective Gospels are complete. Each begins the third chapter of the Gospel as though nothing had preceded it.

Matthew and Luke, furthermore, give us different accounts of the birth. In Matthew alone, we find that Joseph has dreams; Bethlehem seems to be the permanent residence of Mary and Joseph; there are wise men and a star, Herod and a massacre, even Egyptian exile. All of these extraordinary occurrences are missing in Luke. In Luke alone, we find an annunciation to Mary, a family relationship to John the Baptist, a Nazareth residence, a universal census, shepherds, angels in heaven and the references to the inn and the manger.

These striking differences give us some indication that these accounts are theological rather than historical. There are striking differences in the creation accounts of Genesis, the crucifixion accounts of the evangelists, and the Easter stories of

11

the New Testament. The more important an event is in its own right, the less likely it is that the Bible will deal with it factually. Oral cultures find less truth in precise descriptions than writing cultures do. We ourselves probably follow the same pattern when we deal with issues of great personal value. We are less factual and more mythic, less precise and more imaginative when we assess our parents, spouses, children, religious convictions and even our own lives.

We have a tendency to read the infancy stories differently from the way they were intended. We read them with especial attention to the infancy, the virginity of Mary, and the historicity of the occurrences. But the stories are not particularly meant to provide information about any of these details. The point of the infancy narratives is not the infancy but the Christology involved in identifying and accepting the mature Jesus. The virginity of Mary is a theological statement about Jesus rather than a gynecological statement about Mary. It tells us that the Spirit responsible for the ministry and resurrection of Jesus was active in the origins of Jesus and that Jesus must be explained not in terms of human agency alone but in terms that are extraordinary and exceptional. The historicity of the various items in the infancy stories is marginal. These are stories that deal, instead, with symbol and meaning, with theological reflection and cultural continuity. They tell us that the uniqueness of Jesus is not so diverse that he cannot be understood in the context of Jewish life.

And so, Joseph, the father of Jesus, described in the opening chapters of Matthew, is modeled not on the historical Joseph but on the Joseph of Genesis. He too, like Matthew's Joseph, was a dreamer. The Joseph of Genesis is an apt model

12

because his life has similarities to the life of Jesus. He is betrayed by his brothers but forgives them, is thrown into a tomb-like pit and raised back to life, and is not recognized by his own brethren in his new life.

Herod the Great who murders Jewish children is modeled on the pharaoh who murders Jewish children. Moses survives the holocaust just as Jesus will.

Balaam, a Gentile, sees a star and predicts a shepherd-savior for Israel in the future (Num 24). The wise men, Gentiles, see a star and expect the child to become the king of Israel. The stars in the heavens will be paralleled by cosmic disturbances in the death of Jesus. The heavens declare his identity at his birth, as he begins his public ministry in the Jordan and the heavens open, and as he dies in darkness and earthquakes, with the veil of the temple torn open as once the heavens were. The kingship of Jesus is declared not by three gifts of the wise men but after three hours on the cross, which bears the inscription "This is Jesus, the King of the Jews." Later, John will tell us this was done in three languages. "King of the Jews" is a title Matthew uses only twice in his entire Gospel, with the wise men and on the cross, in Bethlehem, David's birthplace, where the child is born, and in Jerusalem, David's city and place of burial, where the young man dies and is buried.

In all of this parrallelism and symbol, the history of Israel is re-enacted, a new Moses and David is presented, and themes of tragedy and triumph are rehearsed in the descriptions of birth and crucifixion. It is the risen Christ, the child of the Spirit, who gives meaning and coherence to the identity of Jesus and to the aspirations of Israel. Indeed, the aspirations are exceeded. For, Israel receives not only a king (which it had before) but a Messiah (which it never had before) and a divine Son of God (which it never anticipated).

The Gospel of Matthew implies that there is a pattern to history, a meaning and a destiny which is not only revealed in Jesus but made invincible in his life. For Jesus is able to be defeated but not destroyed. Jesus, and human history with him, does not only survive. It also prevails.

What does all this mean?

It is Christmas as we begin the Easter triduum. Jesus is born, in poverty, alienated, rejected, besieged, but the birth is depicted in regal terms. He is king of the Jews. There is a star. There are wise men and gifts. Luke speaks of shepherds and songs.

The poverty of the birth is described in royal terms because, later, the poverty of the cross will be delineated in the light of Easter. The birth story has in it the shadows of Calvary and the glory of Easter. The history of this child, from impoverished crib to imperial cross, will be as seamless as the garment taken from him as he was executed. Christmas is suffused with the joy of the child in the manger and the heartache of the children in the massacre. Grace and violence, blessing and bloodshed intermingle. The passion narratives are already begun on the first day of the child's life.

Christmas is the key to Holy Week. We accept the sentiment, emotion and happiness of Christmas profoundly only when we affirm the deep meaning of the events we remember from Holy Thursday to Easter Sunday. The melody of the angels' song of peace on Christmas morning is carried through the greeting of peace on Easter morning by the risen Christ.

There are connections and convergences on endless levels of meaning.

Everything about Jesus is mystery. We, privileged to be his disciples, are invited to decipher in the mystery the meaning of our own life.

The star of Christmas leads us to Calvary. We find Jesus not in the manger but on the cross. The Christmas star is surrounded by the darkness of death but illumined by the light of Easter. This star will become the Easter star on Sunday morning when dawn and daylight mingle together darkness and sunrise.

The starlight of Christmas and the sunshine of Easter are God's Spirit revealing to us God's Son so that we might find meaning in the God who nurtures us as children and rescues us from shipwreck and sorrow. The destiny of Jesus is our own. For this reason, we ourselves are born at Bethlehem and destroyed on Calvary. We ourselves find our way out of the tomb, guided by the star of Easter. In other lives, we behold our own. Biography fascinates us because it is, at its best, autobiography.

When we begin a life journey with Jesus we must go all the way with him if we would find ourselves. We need not only Christmas but the cross in order to understand Christmas and in order to be given Easter.

We are the companions of this child and this crucified savior. If we feel unworthy, we must remember that Jesus, in his birth and in his burial, in the virgin's womb and Calvary's tomb, reverses all expectations. Easter is a return of Christ to those who felt unworthy but who did not stop loving.

We come as wise men and women to the manger, as disciples to the cross, as an Easter people to the empty tomb.

Matthew begins his Gospel with a celebration of Jesus as son of Abraham, son of David, son of Mary, Messiah, Emmanuel, God-is-with-us. The final line of his Gospel is a celebration of us. "And know that I am with you always; yes, to the end of time."

II

Passover

The journey now is from Christmas to Passover. When the Christmas star led us to Bethlehem, the child was about to go away, into Egypt; as we reach Jerusalem and the Passover, the young man is about to go away, to Calvary. It is unsettling to realize how much of absence there is in presence. When the child goes to Egypt and the young man to Calvary, we do not know if he will return nor does anyone tell us how to find him.

We brought the child signs of kingship at Bethlehem; at the end, there are signs of kingship with palms and hosannas. We once gave the child gold and frankincense and myrrh; now the young man washes our feet and gives us bread and wine.

Herod the Great is gone but Caiaphas and Pilate now seek the child. The child is born from the blood and water of Mary's body; Jesus will die as blood and water pour from his side and his mother watches. The blood of Mary leads to the life of Jesus; the blood of Jesus leads to the life of the world. The innocents were slaughtered but Jesus does not die; the blameless paschal Lamb is killed and we live; Israel is saved in the blood of the Lamb and Christians hear unforgettable words spoken over bread and wine.

The swaddling clothes of the manger will become the

winding sheets of the tomb; the perfumes of incense and myrrh for the child become the oils and spices for the dead king. The first sight a mother has of her child's face, the first human touch on a child's body, becomes in the tomb the last look, the last human embrace. Touching is an effort to end the absence and preserve presence.

Passover and Easter enlighten and shape the Christmas story. There are some nights unlike any others, some memories that sustain all those who keep them.

This is a night of memories. The theme now is maturity and memories, parables and Passover.

There is no way to deal with an entire life in a few pages. The life of Jesus has dimensions to it that make such an impossible task all the more unthinkable. Yet we do benefit when we attempt synthesis and understanding. Dealing with the life of Jesus, however inadequately, is enriching.

The memories we have of Jesus include astonishing miracles and fulfilled prophecies, brilliant debates and wrenching confrontations, words that reach the heart, refresh the spirit, heal the whole person. We might gain significant insight into the life by selecting, instead, a few parables and recounting a few stories. We confine ourselves to five passages from Luke. Two of the passages have women as a central concern (the widow of Naim and the Martha-Mary story); two of the passages are parables, perhaps the best Jesus ever devised, each of them found in Luke's Gospel only (good Samaritan and prodigal son); the final selection is Luke's account of the Last Supper.

One of the themes which unify these five passages is compassion. When we find a person who can experience our life

19

deeply enough so as to suffer when we suffer, we encounter compassion (the root meaning of the word). This person becomes, then, our companion (someone we break bread with, the root meaning of "companion"). The bonding in bread and pain creates communion between us (becoming one with each other, the root meaning of "communion"). The compassion of the events and parables leads to the companionship of Jesus with us at the Last Supper and communion with him.

The Widow of Naim

Naim is a two or three hour walk from Nazareth. Jesus must have visited the hamlet often as a youth and a young man. In Naim, as we shall see, Jesus reinforces the present, by confirming the style his ministry is assuming. In Naim, also, the outlines of his own tragic future are delineated.

The story is typical for Luke. The subject and themes are familiar: women, the anonymous, the vulnerable. Jesus brings compassion to an unknown woman whose life resources are depleted. She is a widow, now about to bury her only son. There are few to share her anguish. The ultimate poverty of the poor is the absence of compassion they experience when they hurt. Society regards the pain of the affluent and prominent as something they should not suffer. The poor are expected to grieve.

Jesus has already defined his ministry in terms of the marginalized. It is also a ministry women influence to a remarkable degree. Luke is especially careful to note this.

It is Luke alone who gives us the Magnificat, the pre-Christmas carol sung by Mary while Jesus is still in her womb. No other New Testament writer records the scene for us. The ministry of the future Christ is sketched in that canticle of Mary, his mother. He regards the lowly, feeds the hungry, scatters the proud, shows mercy.

It is Luke alone who gives us this story of the widow of Naim. The Magnificat finds expression in the ministry of Jesus through this miracle story of deep human and symbolic value.

As Jesus and the disciples approach the funeral cortege and its loud weeping, they fall silent. It is late afternoon, the customary time for burial. They see a "dead man . . . carried . . . the only son of his mother . . . a widow." On a distant day in the gathering future, Luke will tell us of another dead man, carried on a cross, the only son of his mother, a widow. The time of his death and burial will be late afternoon.

This story links Jesus with the Magnificat and with Calvary. It also connects with Easter since this will be a resurrection story. In the light of that, Jesus is called "the Lord" here for the first time in Luke's Gospel. It is the Lord who will show compassion and conquer death. "The Lord . . . felt sorry for her," Luke writes. The divine and the human are close in that sentence. "Do not cry," Jesus says.

The funeral procession stops as Jesus touches the bier. Jesus suffers legal impurity by approaching and touching the dead. He endures this for the sake of a woman, because of his compassion, as a way of declaring the character of his ministry.

"Young man, I tell you, get up." Jesus calls the young man from death with words that might well describe how he himself will be summoned from death on Easter morning.

Jesus gives the man to his mother. It is a moment of extraordinary emotion, of disbelief inviting deeper faith, a moment not unlike that the disciples of Jesus experience in Easter.

Jesus heals the young man of death itself. But he also heals the woman, not only of her grief but of her lost social identity. A woman with no man in her life was greatly disadvantaged in ancient Israel.

The response of the crowd is like that of Palm Sunday. Jesus is hailed as a prophet. It is an hour for victory songs, a time when anything is possible, a season when death is banished and life is abundant. It is Christmas and Easter, for a son is born and death gives way to life. But there are shadows in the story. Jesus may be a prophet but prophets are destined to die. The prophet delivers God's word not only with courage but even with his blood.

The story prepares us for Passover. It helps us appreciate what kind of man we are asked to remember in the breaking of the bread. It is a man of compassion who becomes our companion as he invites us to communion with his life. The Lord is indeed the God of mercy who regards the lowly and feeds the hungry. This miracle is the bread of life for a woman in the wilderness of her grief.

Martha and Mary

Martha is the feminine form for "Lord," namely "Lady." Luke tells us that it is *her* house to which Jesus goes. Again, women are made the central concern of a narrative about Jesus.

Martha and Mary are two sisters; later, Luke will give us a story of two brothers, in the parable of the prodigal son. There are other similarities. In both instances, there is a sibling tension, and in both cases the complaint is about being left alone to do work that should be shared. In both accounts, the model to be followed (Mary and the younger brother, respectively) chooses relationship over work. In the Martha-Mary story, Jesus functions in a paternal-parental role; in the prodigal son story, an anonymous person functions as lord, father, parent.

Martha is anxious and angry. She has three complaints against her sister and she brings them not to her sister but to Jesus. Martha complains that she has a great deal of work, that she must do it alone, that Jesus should ask Mary to help.

The elder brother in the other story will also be anxious and angry. He has three complaints against his brother and he brings them not to his brother but to the father. The brother complains that he has worked hard, that he has never disobeyed, that he was never given a party.

In both stories, the reader sympathizes with Martha's dilemma and with the elder brother's plight. There is an element of unfairness here. The narratives, however, as we shall see, are not about sibling equity but about redefinitions of life that go beyond legal justice. Urgent needs must sometimes be addressed not in terms of how others who do not have needs are affected but in terms of the imperatives of the moment. There are times when all the energies of a family must focus on only one member. Equity is dealt with more easily in tranquil moments, when imperatives are less pronounced.

The description Luke offers of the two sisters fits in with the description given later in John's Gospel. The resurrection of Lazarus, in the eleventh chapter, tells us Mary was at the feet of Jesus, anointing them with ointment. She is, of course, at the feet of Jesus, listening, in Luke's account. It is Martha who runs to meet Jesus in John's story and Mary who remains at home.

23

Martha and Mary play this active-passive role in Luke's Gospel. It is Martha who goes to get Mary, in John, and Mary who falls to the feet of Jesus as she greets him. Martha is practical. When Jesus asks that the stone be removed from the tomb of Lazarus, Martha comments on the odor of decay that will follow.

The same character definition of the sisters follow in the twelfth chapter of John. It is Passover season and Martha waits on table at a dinner for her brother, Lazarus, and Jesus. Mary anoints the feet of Jesus. The scene, however, is now dark with tragedy. It is the final Passover in the life of Jesus; the Last Supper will occur in the next chapter. Judas appears in the scene and objects to the waste involved in the anointing. The evangelist notes that Judas was a thief and Jesus justifies the extravagance by saying that the time for his own burial is near. The chief priests conspire to kill Lazarus as they will soon conspire to do away with Jesus.

We are, of course, getting ahead of ourselves. Let us return to Luke's story of Martha and Mary.

Jesus does not accept Martha's account of her predicament. He does not send Mary to do housework with Martha. The point of this non-acceptance is not insensitivity to Martha's dilemma but redefinition of the role women are to play in society. Women were not allowed to be disciples of a rabbi or to sit at the feet of a teacher. Jesus rejects this stereotype and enhances the social condition of women. He does for Mary and also for Martha what he had done for the widow of Naim. He heals the social dignity of the outcast and the marginalized. It is human and gender equity rather than sibling equity which is the issue. If Mary is sent to help Martha, a kind of domestic equity might be maintained but women at large would lose human rights. Mary is praised because she feels free enough to attend to the intellectual and spiritual needs of women, at a time when only men were allowed significant access to learning and religious study.

In these first two portraits of Jesus we have drawn, we begin to see the kind of man he is. Only a man of extraordinary insight and sensitivity would do for a widow and two sisters what Jesus does for them. He is a man of compassion not only for the grief of a bereft widow but for the diminished status in life that has been imposed upon women. Indeed, women have internalized this so that a woman would not expect a holy man to touch her dead son. Nor would women in general dare to sit at the feet of Jesus unless they knew beforehand he would not reject them. Jesus does not say that housework is wrong or ignoble. How could he? He says rather that women are persons with intellectual and spiritual needs which are more imperative than the role society has assigned them.

These two portraits already point in the direction of Calvary. On Calvary, on the cross, Jesus will become the dead son of the widowed mother. On Calvary, in the tomb, Jesus will be already anointed for burial from Mary's ointment. He will be found alive when other women come to the tomb to anoint his feet. He again will break bread with his disciples as he once did with Martha and Mary. This time, however, the bread of companionship will be the Eucharistic banquet. All the disciples will be invited to this table whether they be Jew or Gentile, free or slave, man or woman. For this breaking of bread will be communion not only with the Lord who teaches and at whose feet we learn. This communion will be with the risen Christ and will give rise to everlasting life.

The Good Samaritan

It is a journey of twenty-three miles from Jerusalem to Jericho. The descent along the winding road is a steep one, from 2,250 feet above sea level to 900 feet below it. Jericho was the residential center for the priests of the temple and their families. The parable, therefore, reflects this historical point accurately. It was also a notorious road, an unsafe passage. One had to travel it warily. Indeed, all travel, even within cities, was far more dangerous many centuries ago than it is today.

Jesus uses this setting for another instruction about discipleship. We are not now in the comfortable and affluent home of Martha and Mary. We are on the open road peopled with priests and brigands, Jews and Samaritans, scholars and businessmen.

A man has been robbed and so savagely beaten that he is half dead. He will be left to die not only by the robbers but by "decent" people in the community. Refusal to even inconvenience oneself to help a neighbor in dire need is not a new phenomenon.

A priest passes by, notices the victim and crosses to the other side. Does he leave to avoid the legal impurity of touching an apparently dead man, of coming in contact with blood? Legal purity would be especially urgent if the priest is on his way to the temple. If so, law and liturgy have taken precedence over compassion. Jesus will make much of this theme in his life and preaching. Later, on the cross, another young man, beaten and left half dead, will be ignored by the priests. In this parable, the priest seems to refuse help because legalism or private business is deemed more imperative. A few chapters before, Jesus disregards legalism and

private business for the sake of the bereaved widow of a deceased son. The contrast is unsettling.

The priest who refuses to help the bleeding man reveals to us, by this very action, the nature of the God he affirms. It is a God of law rather than mercy.

The indictment of institutional religion when it betrays human values is intensified by the second person who travels the road. This is a Levite, a temple official, someone involved with liturgy and worship. He too passes by, also "on the other side," trying to get as far as possible from the man. Human needs have a way of complicating religious systems. Those who make choices of system over person remove themselves from their neighbors' care. The parable is an answer to one of those haunting biblical questions: "And who is my neighbor?" The neighbor is defined in terms of need.

And now a layman comes upon the dying man. The layman is even further removed from Jewish institutional religion by the fact that he is a Samaritan; he is, in effect, a religious heretic. He and the dying Jew had been raised to hate each other. There are other reasons to prompt non-involvement. Samaritans are ethnically impure, not only a culture that has betrayed religious values but one whose history and identity are offensive to Jews. There are religious and social, historical and psychological, cultural and personal reasons to abandon the victim. It is unsafe to stop on the open road. The dying man would be hostile to care given by a Samaritan. The Samaritan has urgent business to attend to; one did not travel for frivolous reasons in the ancient world. To stop and help one so sorely in need will require hours, perhaps days.

The only claim the dying man has on the Samaritan is their

common humanity. The Samaritan answers two age-old questions as he puts aside his own concerns for the sake of another. He has decided that he is his brother's keeper, and that the neighbor is the one who needs us. The parable is an answer to a lawyer's question about who is his neighbor. The Samaritan shows himself to be a man of compassion, one who enters into the suffering of another. The response he makes is not a religious or an ethnic response as such but a human one.

As compassion becomes concrete, it also becomes sacramental. The Samaritan does not feel compassion from afar but touches the wounded man. He cleanses him with wine (an antiseptic) and anoints him with oil (a curative). He bandages the wounds. He lifts him onto his own mount and carries him to an inn. It is a dangerous, difficult, demanding display of compassion. This time there is room in the inn; when Jesus was born, there was none.

The God revealed by the unorthodox Samaritan is the true God of Israel, a God of mercy rather than law. The layman has become a priest in this sacrifice of himself and in his witness to the true God. Later, the young man who now tells us the parable, the layman Jesus, will become a priest, when he too is lifted up, when he will make a sacrifice of himself and become the good Samaritan for all of us, a faithful witness to the true God of love. On the cross, the compassion of God will be revealed in the Son; on the open road, the compassion of God is revealed in the Samaritan.

The kindness continues. Luke tells us that the Samaritan looked after him, that he stayed overnight, that he left two denari (about $100) to see that the man was given attention. He did all this for a total stranger, for an enemy. The Samaritan then has to leave; he is, perhaps, on a business trip; the business is urgent; he can stay no longer; but he will soon return. He tells the innkeeper that he will pay whatever else was required to care for the sick man.

Who of the three was the neighbor? Jesus raises the question immediately after the story. How different questions sound when they are no longer theoretical! The lawyer who began all this with an abstract question hears the question again after a concrete human experience has been described. Now, it is not Jesus but the lawyer who is tested.

The test is severe. The Samaritan lacks dignity and status. How does a lawyer opt publicly for a Samaritan over his own priests and Levites, over his own people? And yet, how could one possibly choose the insensitivity of the Jewish priest over the extravagant love of the lay Samaritan? Humanity transcends religious and cultural barriers. Behavior exceeds doctrine. The dying Jewish man is safer in the hands of someone who is human to the core than he is in the hands of those who administer an institution, and who have betrayed their humanity for a contrived orthodoxy.

The lawyer cannot bring himself to use the word "Samaritan." He answers the question correctly but reluctantly: the one who takes pity on the beaten man is the neighbor, he says. The lawyer is forced to choose between the human heart and heartless institutional leaders. He knows the heart is braver. He chooses for all of us. And Jesus approves.

There is an epilogue to the parable. It occurs as we reflect on the consequences of the story. When the beaten Jewish man recovered and asked how he got there and who brought him, he would have been shocked to learn it was a Samaritan. Now the physical healing becomes a spiritual healing. The stereotypes of an entire race would have been discredited. How difficult it would be to harbor the hatred of the past. One also marvels at the spiritual maturity of the Samaritan who had grown beyond social conditioning and selfish concerns to reach out in generosity and extravagance.

There are also analogues in the parable. Jesus himself will be beaten on the open road outside Jerusalem. He will be stripped and robbed of life, left to die. There will be no good Samaritan, once again no inn to receive him. There will not even be wine. He will be given vinegar. No priest or Levite will offer compassion.

The stories of Jesus tell us a great deal about himself. The things Jesus does etch the memory of him indelibly into our consciousness. A man who would touch and heal the grief of a widow at Naim, a man who would redefine the role of women against the prejudice his own society engendered, a man who would indict his own religious establishment and exalt humanity even in the form of a rejected people, such a man would be unforgettable. The memory of a man like Jesus would be healing. The memory of his deeds and stories would be worth repeating and retelling. Such a man would be celebrated for as long as people cared about the human heart and one another. The memory of this man is already liturgy, clearly sacramental. The preservation of the significance of such a man's life preserves all of us.

The Prodigal Son

There are no geographical coordinates for this parable as there were for that of the good Samaritan or for the events of

Naim or the home of Martha and Mary. The landscape of this story is psychological; the cosmology of this world is profoundly human.

The opening line is arresting: "A man had two sons." The anonymity invites us to take the place of the participants; the family references stir universal longings and specific identities.

The good Samaritan and the prodigal son—Jesus may never have told better stories. And yet only Luke records them. What a good, sensitive man Jesus must have been! To have crucified such a brave and gentle storyteller criss-crosses us with grief and guilt. Had we been there we might not have done better than those who twisted the meaning of the stories and tormented the storyteller until his body could bear no more pain. How prodigal we were with the untold value of such a life!

If we knew nothing about Jesus, only these stories, we would know most of what there is to know about him. Even the regal trappings of the Christmas story do not do him as much honor as these parables.

The parable of the prodigal son is a parable about all of us. It is a story about those who have wasted life in some ways and who need to be forgiven for this. The waste may have occurred as we made a bad use of time or opportunities, of love or trust, of people or projects. We break faith with life at times; we need someone to set us free from the wrong decisions, their unhappy consequences and the regrets that accompany them.

But this is a story not only about a son who went astray but, more especially, about a father whose love had no limits.

The best gift a father gives is the memory he instills in his children. In this, a father gives life even after he is gone.

The memory of Jesus is the best of his gifts to us. As long as we remember, Jesus gives life. Tonight, Holy Thursday, is a night of memories; Passover is worth celebrating because the memories revitalize and renew. How could we have forgotten Jesus in human history and judged ourselves human or good anymore! The worst of our sins is the refusal to keep alive the memories we need to continue and to grow. Tonight we do things in memory of Jesus for the sake of everyone. We take mere bread and wine, but embedded in these elements is the presence that only memory gives.

As we break bread, we are in Naim and a youthful Jesus brings us to life even as we are carried out for burial. This is a night for widows and bereaved parents to rejoice. As we break bread, we are at the home of Martha and Mary and a young teacher tells us the unforgettable words we long to hear. As we listen, we sense in our souls a trembling that goes with joy and freedom and love and ecstasy. This is a night for sisters and brothers to quarrel no more, a night for friends, a night to be passed in our homes, in peace. As we break bread, an enemy picks up a broken man and holds him until he is healed, until he can see sunrise for another day and count the stars for one more night. If there are no friends left on the road of life, no enemies who become companions when we need them most, what is life for, who would want to endure it? This is a night when the human heart makes all strangers members of the family, a night when every face and name seems familiar, when no one doubts whether others are with us. As we break bread, every father and mother searches for their children, every son and daughter comes back, every home is filled with music and forgiveness. This is a night when the lost are found and our hands hold for a moment all the beautiful things that once slipped away. On this night, a young man will assure us that nights like this are the bread and body of life, the wine and blood of the human spirit. Someone must sing a song for all of us; someone must fashion a memory all can share; someone must be companion for everyone; someone must put bread in our hands when they are empty and wine in the drained chalice of our hearts.

Somewhere, on every road, the father who forgives the prodigal child waits.

The younger son in the parable is not married; he is less than twenty years of age. This is also true of the elder brother. They are young men, brothers, whose relationship is uneasy; they are the counterparts of the sisters, Martha and Mary, who often disagree. This parable happens out of doors, in the fields; it contrasts with the domestic setting of the Martha-Mary story. It has similarities with the Cain and Abel story. There, too, the elder brother renounces the younger brother; there, too, the story occurs in the fields.

The father is affluent; Jesus did not believe that only the economically poor were virtuous. The father is poor in another way; he needs people, needs his sons, needs to give life, to keep nothing. The younger son asks for his share of the estate; he does not wait until the father dies. He wants to get away, with all the assets he can acquire. Jewish custom stipulated that he was entitled to a third of the estate provided that he renounce all future claims. It was a lot of money for a teenager. It was a heartache for the father. It was as though a price had been placed on the father's head. Years of love for nothing! Moneygiver, not life-giver! Over the centuries, the pattern would repeat itself.

The initial exuberance, the first sense of freedom is short-lived. It was not long before he had spent it all. And now there was famine. The poor know better how to survive. This young man never experienced hunger, poverty, social neglect, anonymity. The prostitutes were not friendly when they were no longer paid. He seeks a job for the first time in his life. He is given responsibility to feed pigs. The last coins of his self-esteem are bartered.

Jewish law cursed the man who raised swine. The young man is given such a task. He is willing to eat the husks the pigs are given for food. The husks of the carob tree were eaten as a sign of penance.

The landscape of the young man's life is bleak. It is a cruel April, a human and spiritual wasteland. He begins to wonder as so many do, when their fortunes fail, about the enormity of their sins and crimes. He begins to believe he is not only destitute but actually evil. He feels unworthy on every level of his life.

And now the memories return. It is all we finally leave with those we love. The memory of the father makes him feel human once more. The father creates the son a second time, this time with the passion of memory, with the passion of compassion. The one future claim the young son knew he had not renounced was the claim of love. The father was the kind of man who made forgiveness, even in incredible circumstances, believable. For the first time, the son realizes how much damage he must have caused to another life. Even without the father's presence, the memory of the father assures him he will never be an orphan. All his life he will be part of a family.

35

The courage it takes to return, to ask for forgiveness, to face the man you yourself left half-dead on the road to Jericho!

"Father, I have sinned against you." What it must have meant to the father to hear his son call him again!

It took a lot of time to spend that much money. And the father waited. Every day he looked down the road that took his son away. Would he die without ever seeing his son again? Every day is so many days!

The son feels unworthy of the father. Love is a paradox of daring and diffidence. We feel unworthy before the manger, at the Lord's supper, as our feet are washed, near the cross, in the empty tomb, on the shore of Galilee as Easter light reveals the forgiver.

The father runs to "the boy." It is the way a parent sees children, whatever the age.

Jewish custom would not permit a father to take the initiative in such a case. The father not only runs, he clasps his son and kisses him "tenderly." The boy's first word is "father." Was it ever easier or harder to use the word?

The son says in effect: "I desire nothing. I'm nobody. Just don't hate me or turn away." It is the language of defeat, uttered when all resources and even one's very self have been devalued.

The father does not allow the son to finish his speech. He is lavish in his response. He reverses the vocabulary and symbols of slavery. The boy is not a servant but "this son of mine"; he is to wear not work clothes but "the best robes"; there is to be no yoke of submission but a ring of bonding and love; he is to have sandals on his feet rather than the bare feet of the hireling. A feast is ordered; a special calf is prepared; there is to be celebration because the dead son is now alive, the lost child is found, the one who once rejected the father has returned and is restored.

There is an Easter element in the story. Jesus will one day be the dead son now alive, the lost who is found. He will return, to the indescribable joy of the disciples.

There is another dimension to the parable we have yet to consider. The elder son is on his way back from the fields and hears the music and the dancing. He has not heard the sounds of celebration in the house for a long time.

One can understand the chagrin of the elder brother, just as one could understand the plight of Martha in the Martha-Mary story. Human circumstances are seldom capable of easy resolution. The forgiveness we extend to one person sometimes offends another.

The elder brother is correct. The younger brother has acted outrageously. He may almost have killed his father with grief. The affluence of the family has not been easily come by and now a great deal of it has been squandered. Furthermore, the younger brother did not go out to the elder for forgiveness and, in any case, no one came into the fields to summon him home.

The music and the anger are contrasted. The elder brother is confronted with celebration and justice. He is correct; he has a legitimate complaint. Not only forgiveness but celebration is expected of him. He chooses vengeance and resentment and makes a plausible case. The Church will often be presented with the same alternative.

The father judges differently. Justice may be proper but it will not save and heal the young boy. The second son has been so devastated that only an extravagant gesture will rescue him. The father considers not what is due to himself but what the younger brother needs.

Jesus is sensitive to the complexities of family life. The father is parent of both sons. He comes out of the house to speak with his first-born; once again, he takes the initiative; this would have surprised his contemporaries, many of whom would have disapproved. Like Jesus, the father resists custom and law when love is the issue.

The elder son spits out his anger and attacks the father rather than his brother. It is one of the perils of forgiveness.

The son accuses the brother to the father rather than face-to-face. Parents are often caught in just such a web. He calls his brother "this son of yours," rejecting all ties of affection and blood. He becomes the lawyer who once asked a question of Jesus rather than the Samaritan of whom Jesus spoke in reply. The haunting questions are still with us. "Am I my brother's keeper?" "Who is my neighbor?" "Lord, how often must I forgive my brother if he wrongs me? As often as seven times?"

The older son never uses the word "father." He begins his speech harshly, "Look." He wants his brother to be accused properly, punished appropriately. "He and his women . . . "

The response of the father is extraordinary. In the Greek, he calls his son "teknon," "my child," a term of exquisite affection. "All I have is yours."

In effect, he invites the son into Passover. He coaxes him to get beyond the anger and the justice, the bitterness and the equity. How can we not celebrate? The boy has suffered enough. He has been crucified and left without a friend in the world. Now, he has no one but us.

The father knows what it is like to be isolated. He is, no doubt, a widower and has lived too long without one of his sons. Now he wishes to break bread with his family, to get beyond the enmity and the death, to give a new spirit to those he loves, to share wine and to assure them they will not be left as orphans.

The Passover Supper

The Passover Supper begins in the circle of actions and stories that make Jesus unforgettable. The disciples gather with memories of a widow of Naim who will not be alone this Passover, with visions of Martha and Mary in Bethany who have heard the word of God and kept it. Jesus is word and life for those who join him in this Last Supper. He has preached the Gospel to the women and the poor; he has brought the dead to life.

The Passover Supper gives the parables flesh and blood. It is celebrated with the wine poured by the Samaritan on the wounds of a young Jewish man, with the bread broken for a prodigal son. The wine of love and the bread of mercy are Passover symbols for the world, parables of compassion for the Christian community.

The Passover account in Luke begins ominously. Some Jewish leaders seek the death of the story-teller. Satan enters Judas.

In the fourth chapter of his Gospel, Luke tells us that Satan left Jesus, alone, in the desert, at the beginning of his ministry. He would, however, "return at the appointed time." The appointed time has come.

Luke is ominous but gentle. Judas is not described as "betraying" Jesus, as he is in Mark; he is not selling Jesus, as Matthew portrays him; he is not called a "thief" as he is in John. He is a more passive character in a larger drama and a more intense hostility. It is Satan who is responsible for the arrest of Jesus.

Judas approaches the priests and the temple police. The police were chosen from Levites. And so, in some ways, the good Samaritan parable comes to life: priests and Levites will do nothing to prevent the death of a fellow Jew, indeed they actively seek it. And Judas, one of the twelve, becomes the prodigal son who wastes his inheritance and squanders love. Judas, as we know from the other evangelists, does not return. He remains outside the circle of the twelve, much as did the elder brother in the parable. And, in his anger and grief, he dies there.

Peter and John are sent into the city to prepare for Passover. They will later emerge as the two most prominent of the twelve in the formation of early Christian community. This Passover dinner will become a focal point in that early community's life and the two major apostles who surround Jesus prepare that event.

It is a last supper, a time for final, brave words.

Luke describes Jesus as affectionate and melancholy. "I have longed to eat this Passover with you before I suffer." Later, he confides "You stood by me faithfully in my trials; and now I confer a kingdom on you."

It is a night as tender and tragic as Christmas. Life and love are multiplied but death divides the abundance inexorably. A child is born but Herod and hatred, violence and exile remind us that all is not well. Jesus gathers his disciples, but there is talk of suffering and treachery, of absence and grief.

Never before did Jesus speak as he did that night. John captures the verbal and emotional intensity of that evening most fully. Jesus uses the affectionate name for the disciples that the father had used in the parable of the prodigal son. He calls them "teknia" in Greek, "my little children." He tells them to love one another, words a dying parent might say to all the remaining children. He says words the father might have shared with the returning prodigal: words of peace, of not being troubled in heart, words telling them they are not servants in the kingdom but friends. "You are in me and I am in you." Compassion has become communion on its most intense level. They are vine and branches, one life, one mystical body. It is a night of indelible memories, invincible love, and enduring life.

And now bread is broken, "my body for you"; and a new community is announced, baptized, "in my blood for you." Only Luke, among the evangelists, has Jesus ask that this action be done "in memory of me." As the community relives this moment in the near future, it will remember the cross and Easter as well as the parables and miracles. The words of this night will become the body and blood of the speaker.

The shadows deepen. The hand of the betrayer is on the table; friendship and faithfulness intermingle. No disciple is immune. Peter will not betray but he will deny. Luke again tells us that Satan is the adversary, that Peter will be sifted like wheat. Peter will bring to Jesus not three gifts but three denials. Christmas will be reversed. It is a dark night. Luke is the only evangelist to tell us that Judas and Peter fail Jesus *after* the bread has been broken, the wine shared, the memory of this night evoked and consecrated.

41

And now something almost impossible to imagine occurs. The disciples argue about power and privilege. Judas betrays in despair; Peter denies in fear. Somehow these are lesser sins. The greater sin is to lord it over others. It will be the Church's greatest temptation, its fatal flaw, its worst hour. It surfaces on this most unlikely occasion. Jesus tells the disciples that all ministry is service, that love is the only authority we have over one another, that he spent his life as a servant.

In John's Gospel, Jesus does more. He kneels at the feet of his friends, washing them, performing the task of a slave. A woman had once done this for him with tears and oil. He wraps their feet and dries them, the way Mary must once have wrapped him in swaddling clothes, the way an anonymous Samaritan once bandaged a beaten man.

On this night of memories, there must be no memories of authority, only the service of love.

The upper room in Jerusalem is also the manger of Bethlehem. The gifts given the child at Christmas are returned at Passover. There are three of them: bread and wine and washing. The manger which holds the mystery of Christmas and Passover is now ourselves, the community consecrated to remember. We are to offer the gifts received to all those who need, even if they be prodigal children or enemies left to die on the open road, beyond Jerusalem.

III

A Paschal Homily

It is the last supper of his life. He is aware of this. The disciples know that he is passing from them and that he will be less easy to find in the future.

Bread and wine are shared as they have never been before. The memories of Jesus are indelibly embedded in the breaking and drinking. The disciples gather all the fragments and pieces of that night, hoping to make Jesus whole by faith and memory.

This night is different from other nights. Through the centuries, bread and wine will have new meanings because of this night. This will be the longest night in the world's history, extended into Friday's crucifixion, and into the darkness that seals the tomb on Calvary. It is a night that still goes on whenever the disciples break open their hearts for the sake of new life or receive into their spirits the wine of expanded love.

This night is different because Jesus washes the feet of his friends. He kneels, as countless numbers kneeled before him, and he takes the part of a slave. He washes the feet of his friends in a last effort to teach those who believe in him the nature of the community they ought to have with one another. The washing is a sacramental and ecclesial action. If we encounter Jesus in bread and wine, we encounter the Church in

the service of washing. The Church is Christ's community when it renounces power. We wash one another's feet so that people may walk freely from us, on their own two feet, if they wish. A slave has no claim on free men and women.

Peter protests the washing. But Peter needs the washing most of all. He must learn that the first apostle is the one who gives an unparalleled example of freedom. Jesus tells them that they call him "Master" and "Lord" and yet he washes their feet. As Jesus takes the place of a slave, he sets all slaves free. This is a night of freedom and a night of love; they are the same thing. Jesus gives the three great Christmas gifts that announce the birth of the Church—the bread of love, the wine of the spirit, the washing of freedom. Such a holy night! O holy night!

As the candle light grows dim and the Christmas stars of creation are lighted, as the paschal lamb becomes one with us, as the bread is in our hands and the wine warms our hearts, the Master kneels before each one of us and washes our feet. In a few hours, his feet will be nailed to the cross. But such a nailing is an act of power. And power will not hold him.

He washed our feet! How can we lord it over others when the Lord washed our feet?

And so, is it any wonder that we give one another bread and wine tonight? We offer words of forgiveness and signs of peace. We wash one another's feet. Friends do such things. There are no masters and servants, no lords and slaves. Tonight, in the Church, we are all friends.

As we do these things, we find Jesus again and we discover that Easter is already here in the washing. As Christ pours his Spirit upon us as flowing water, our baptism commits us to the meaning of this Supper and of the events to follow on Friday and Sunday. Tonight, the water that washes our feet is an initiation rite into these three days. Like all commitments, we do not realize all that is at issue at the time we make them. But as we wash one another's feet through the centuries, we shall learn.

One day, as the Passover candles and Christmas stars of our own life grow dim, as we enter the darkness of our own death, as we prepare with bread and wine, baptismal water and final anointings for the passage from this life, we shall find him at our feet. Recalling the misdeeds of a lifetime and sensing as never before how weak we are, we shall protest, "Lord, are you going to wash my feet?" Jesus will assure us that it is what a friend does for a friend. Only then shall we know how strong the bonds of love are. As we kneel to wash the feet of Jesus, we shall see his face. We shall see in the Christmas light more than the magi beheld; we shall find in the Easter glory more than the Last Supper disciples perceived. It will not be our last supper but our final night in this world. The Jesus who washes our feet tells us he has prepared a home for us, one we had not found until now. And he will take us there.

IV

Gethsemane to Grave

It is Friday. This is no time for Christmas. In any case, the star is not visible. Bethlehem seems to have been another country, another century. The magi are absent; the gifts are gone; Joseph is dead.

Herod remains, in the son of Herod who rules in Galilee. Egypt remains, in the brutal Roman soldiers. The innocent are still put to death.

The beauty and poetry of Christmas have dimmed; the dark shadows of the story dominate.

The widow of Naim is not here, nor her son but both will learn of what came to pass. A widow *is* here and her son is on the cross.

Martha and Mary no longer hear the Master's voice. The parables are over, those wonderful stories. Jesus tells us no more.

The good Samaritan is on the cross, crucified by those he helped on the road.

The two sons of the forgiving father are not here but there are two robbers, one with the anger of the elder brother, the other with the remorse of the prodigal son. The father of the parable is on the cross now, his arms still open to receive his lost children. Now, of course, he cannot run to greet his grieving son and so the son must come to the cross for pardon.

Such wonderful stories. We did not know when he told them that they were about himself. How could we know that the child of Christmas and the storyteller would come to this?

The father of the parable gave his son a robe and sandals. And now the father is on the cross, his robe torn, his sandals gone. The father who would not allow the son to become a slave is now himself a slave on the cross. But the words of forgiveness go on.

He gave us wine at the Last Supper and now he is offered vinegar. He who washed our feet has no water for his thirst.

Gethsemane

A few hours earlier, Jesus was in Gethsemane. The accounts of what happened in that garden vary.

In Mark, the scene is especially bleak, with the typical starkness of that evangelist. Jesus is alone, in the dust; the disciples sleep although roused by Jesus on three occasions. Judas receives no word of greeting; the sword is drawn but there is no healing. A disciple runs away naked when a soldier seizes his linen cloak. Once the disciples were asked to leave all and follow Jesus; now they leave all in a desire to desert.

Matthew offers other details, with strong references, as he is fond of doing, to Jewish history. Jesus comes to the Mount of Olives. Zechariah (14:4) had written that the last day in the world would begin when God descended on the Mount of Olives, bringing blessings and judgment. Luke will describe the ascension of Jesus from the Mount of Olives.

The Mount of Olives links Jesus with some of the tragic

history of David (2 Sam 15:30–31). David makes his way to the Mount, weeping, his head covered, his feet bare. David weeps because his family and friends have betrayed him. Absalom, his son, and Ahitophel conspire against him. Ahitophel hangs himself as the conspiracy misfires.

Jesus enters this historic place of judgment and sorrow. He suffers the imminent execution on a psychological level, in Gethsemane, before he endures it with his own flesh and blood. He senses that every avenue of escape is closed.

The stress is so intense that Luke tells us his sweat fell to the ground like great drops of blood. Only Luke speaks of an angel coming to console Jesus; Luke alone had described an angel in the annunciation which began the Christmas story. The angel of the annunciation told Mary not to fear, that a child would be born to her; the angel of consolation strengthens Jesus as the end of that life conceived in the Spirit approaches.

Luke's account of the annunciation gives us words of the angel that seem especially fitting for consolation now. The angel announces: "The Lord is with you . . . do not be afraid, you have won God's favor . . . nothing is impossible to God." The response of Mary to the annunciation is similar to the acceptance of Jesus in his agony. She says: "I am the handmaid of the Lord . . . let what you have said be done to me." Jesus prays: "Father . . . let your will be done, not mine." The conception of Jesus and the crucifixion, the beginning and the end, will be inspired by God's Spirit.

Jesus arises from prayer fortified; the disciples sleep, Luke compassionately notes, not from indifference but from "sheer grief."

John's Gospel portrays a Jesus in command of his destiny.

There is no agony in the garden, only an arrest. Jesus is not startled by those who seize him; he knew "everything that was going to happen to him." Jesus is not prostrate in the dust, as in Mark, but his captors fall to the ground as Jesus declares, "I am he." The Gethsemane experience is a divine apparition, an annunciation of origins and identity, rather than a night of anguish and torment.

It is dark in the garden, despite the Passover moon. The captors do not come with swords and clubs only, as they do in Matthew and Mark, but with lanterns and torches. These, however, do not enlighten them about Jesus of Nazareth. It is Jesus who is the only light in that deep darkness. He asks that all his disciples be set free even as he submits to captivity. He is ready "to drink the cup that the Father has given me."

The drama which begins the passion narrative is an intriguing blend of the divine and the human. The human desolation is most graphically depicted by Mark; the divine implications are most clearly drawn by John. The themes of distress, betrayal and destiny link all the accounts and make them harmonious. In the garden, Jesus is both distraught and resolute, fearful and confident, grieved and resigned. He is crushed by sorrow on the Mount of Olives, so that we might be anointed with the oil of gladness. He is weighed down by agony in the wine press of Gethsemane (the meaning of the name) so that we might be renewed with the chalice of salvation.

Sanhedrin

The Sanhedrin trial is the first of the three judicial ordeals. Jerusalem, Galilee (Herod), and Rome (Pilate) will deal with the accused officially before the sentence of death is administered.

The purpose of the three proceedings is not so much a concern about guilt, innocence or civil rights but mostly a concern with making the execution sufficiently legal. A religious decision (Sanhedrin), a Jewish civil decision (Herod) and an imperial decision (Pilate) will concur in the fact that there is positive evidence or "no cause to deny" the execution.

It is a fearful thing to kill a human being ritualistically. At points in the process, the ritual becomes more imperative than justice or mercy. It is ironic that a man who spoke of spirit rather than law, of love rather than ritual, should be destroyed with such careful attention to law and such impeccable ritual.

The trials of Jesus represent a never-ending story of using the law to justify immorality or ritual to substitute for humaneness or administrative judgments to crush the human spirit. Even in religious institutions, one finds in the course of history a repetition of the same pattern.

To stand before accusers who have the power to execute and who have an utterly different life perspective is terrifying. The innocence of Jesus will not be declared in these proceedings. In Gethsemane, Jesus had his trial, so to speak, before his own conscience and before God. On that level, before such a forum, Jesus is not guilty.

In Mark's Gospel, the verdict from the Sanhedrin is that the accused deserves to die. It is a unanimous verdict. The justification for the capital offense is blasphemy. There is a triple shock in this result: death, unanimity, blasphemy. It is not only death but the degradation of the charge of blasphemy and the universal support of it which takes from the accused the last shreds of human respect.

Jesus is condemned and then derided. Before the high

court of his own people, he is spit upon, blindfolded, beaten with fists, mocked as a prophet ("Play the prophet!").

By contrast, the Passover meal and the prayer of Gethsemane seem ineffectual.

Jesus might easily have wondered about who would remember a life coming to such an ignominious end. Where is the star? The magi? It hardly seems the same life, begun with gifts of gold and myrrh, filled with stories of compassion and freedom, marked with the miracles of healing and glory. He who but hours before washed the feet of his own followers has no one to wash his face and hands.

The other evangelists offer few other details about the Sanhedrin trial. Matthew, in his typical fashion, gives references to Jewish history. The temple figures more decisively in the case against Jesus. At a time when Jewish identity is threatened by Greek culture and Roman rule, the symbols of the nation are clung to staunchly. Preeminent among these symbols are temple and Torah. Jesus is accused of finding the destruction of the temple acceptable and of violating the Torah with blasphemy. Jeremiah (26:1–15), at a less troubled time than this, had been told he deserved to die because he prophesied that the temple would be destroyed. At Jeremiah's trial, he declared that "if you put me to death, you will be bringing innocent blood on yourselves, on this city."

The Sanhedrin trial of Jesus reaches its decisive moment, not in the verdict, but in the tearing of the garments of the high priest. Such an action indicated that the Torah had been violated. The fact that the chief priest does this, before the high court of Israel, makes everything else in the trial anti-climactic.

Luke adds a touching detail to the proceedings of that fateful night. He is the only evangelist to tell us that, as Peter denies Jesus, "The Lord turned and looked straight at Peter." It is a tragic and heartbreaking scene. Luke alone adds the sad but saving observation that Peter "went outside and wept bitterly."

John does not describe a Sanhedrin trial, but an interrogation before Annas.

It is never an easy experience to be judged guilty of an ultimate crime and to be given a terminal penalty. When one's own nation charges treason and imposes exile, or one's own religious community charges sacrilege and excommunicates, it is the very spirit of the accused that is indicted, the very presence of the accused that is deemed offensive. Jesus, before the trials are over, will be branded with treason and sacrilege, with betrayal and blasphemy. He will be excommunicated, exiled and executed. The execution will be the most degrading and painful execution allowed under law.

Herod

Compared to the great trials before Jerusalem and Rome, the interrogation before Herod is an interlude. It is mentioned only in Luke.

Luke begins the public ministry of Jesus with a reference to Herod, the tetrarch of Galilee. He closes the public ministry before Herod. This Herod is not Herod the Great who acts in the infancy narratives of Matthew. This Herod is his son, Herod Antipas. Antipas ruled Galilee during the entire lifetime of Jesus. Jesus, therefore, heard much about him as he grew into maturity.

Matthew's Herod was responsible for the slaughter of the innocents. The son is like the father. Herod Antipas will de-

54

capitate John the Baptist and will treat Jesus of Galilee with contempt. Earlier, he had sought to kill Jesus (Lk 13:31).

Herod the Great finally meets Jesus, in the person of his son. The son seeks the death of Jesus, as his father has done. This time the blood of Jesus will be shed but, in an even more startling manner, Jesus will elude Herod, not with the Christmas star but with the Easter sunrise.

Luke recounts the sanguinary history of the Herods. He alone will tell us of the grandson of Herod the Great, Herod Agrippa I, who will decapitate James, one of the twelve, the brother of John the evangelist. Agrippa will arrest Peter and try to kill him. The great-grandson of Herod the Great, Herod Agrippa II, will be crucial in the trial of Paul, a trial that will lead him to Rome where he will be decapitated. And so the Herods leave a trail of blood across the road traveled by Jesus and the early Christian community.

Luke observes that Herod and Pilate were enemies until the day Jesus is crucified. The enmity may have been caused by Pilate's brutality in slaughtering Galileans (Lk 13:1), during the time when Herod rules Galilee. The diplomatic nicety of sending the accused to Herod helps Pilate heal the breach.

In any case, the death of an innocent man leads those in power to respect each other. It will not be the last time human life is sacrificed for institutional priorities.

The Roman Trial

For Pilate, there is one key question about Jesus that needs an answer. "Are you the King of the Jews?" Blasphemy against the God of Israel would not trouble a Roman official; political pretensions, sedition or insurrection would assure a response.

Mark does not use the title "King of the Jews" until this moment in the Gospel. The question, therefore, reflects the interest and anxieties of the Romans.

There are a number of psychological currents in the trial. Pilate marvels at the silence of Jesus in the face of accusations against him. He objects to the death sentence because he fails to find evidence to support it. He eventually orders the destruction of a human life because he wants to please the crowd.

The portrait is not a flattering one. Yet, the four evangelists provide a more sympathetic description of Pilate than that given by Philo, a contemporary, and Josephus, a first century historian. They describe Pilate as obstinate, violent, cruel and greedy. The evangelists collectively portray him as torn between the crowd and Caesar, as offering choices other than execution, as protesting the innocence of the accused. Pilate emerges as unprincipled and weak, willing to send the innocent to death to preserve his power. Yet his reluctance to act as he does and his feeble efforts to make a difference are not unnoteworthy.

Matthew adds one note of mingled grace and shame. Pilate washes his hands of responsibility for the decision he alone had responsibility to make. The Book of Deuteronomy (21:6–9) describes a ritual washing of hands by which innocence of murder is signified.

Pilate's dilemma is compounded in Matthew's Gospel by the intervention of his wife. She, a Gentile woman, has had a dream which assures her that there is something extraordinary about Jesus. On an earlier occasion, the Gentile magi were led by star and dreams to the extraordinary child at Christmas. It is Matthew alone who gives us these accounts of revelation to the Gentiles in dreams. They mark the beginning and the end of the history of Jesus. The dreams link Herod and Pilate, a link that runs through the early literature of the Christian era.

The Johannine account of the Roman trial is a study in ironies and reversals. The light and darkness contrast of John's description of Gethsemane is now made a contrast of tumult and tranquility. The crowds demand death for Jesus and scream for the release of Barabbas, outside the praetorium. They remain outside lest they be legally defiled by entering a Gentile building. Inside, the dialogue between Pilate and Jesus is calm and quiet. Jesus is inside a Gentile residence, once again legally defiled and yet religiously liberated. Jesus is eloquent and triumphant before Pilate in the praetorium, as he was before Annas in the high priest's palace. A series of reversals ensues in John's description. In the interrogation before Annas, Jesus asks the key questions so that the interrogators are interrogated. In the trial before Pilate, it is Pilate who is put on trial.

All four evangelists name Barabbas and describe the choice the crowds make. Barabbas means "son of the father"; he is selected for freedom while Jesus, "Son of God," is to be killed.

The Roman soldiers now become brutal with the condemned man. The Sanhedrin had already insulted Jesus with fists and spitting and cries of "Play the prophet." The soldiers force Jesus to play the king with a crown of thorns, a colored cloak, a reed in his hand. He is given "homage" with cries of "Hail" followed by spitting and striking. Both Jew and Gentile degrade the man for whom death is not enough.

Crucifixion

There would never be a death quite like this one, just as there had never been such a birth. There were no clinical descriptions of Christmas; there would be none of Calvary. Physical detail misses the significance of both events. Some of the richest symbols human history knows would be utilized for description; centuries of reflection would not exhaust the mystery or trivialize the majesty of Bethlehem and Jerusalem.

Mary is a link between both events although there are no recorded words from her. Mothers have little or nothing to say at the birth or death of their children. The silent joy and grief of Mary universalize her experience more effectively than words. She will become, in later history, an unparalleled example of virginity and motherhood, of widowhood and Pietà. All the gain and loss of life will happen in her arms where she holds both Christmas and the Crucified.

Crucifixion was an Oriental form of punishment, introduced into the West by the Persians. It was seldom used by the Greeks but it was extensively utilized by the Romans. The Romans reserved the cross for slaves and for those not citizens of the Empire. Cicero stated accurately the Roman assessment of crucifixion as the "most cruel and repulsive of punishments." It is not mentioned in the Hebrew Scriptures.

Jesus was probably crucified on a *crux immissa* or dagger-shaped cross. This is suggested by the fact that a title is affixed above his head. This would not be possible with a *crux commissa* or T-shaped cross.

The condemned carried the crossbeam to the place of crucifixion, where the upright beam was left permanently in place. The arms of the crucified were fastened and he was elevated to the upright beam. Ropes and nails were used since nails would not support the weight of the body. Four nails were used and ropes were tied around arms, legs and torso. The ropes prevented the victim from tearing himself loose. Most of the weight of the body was supported on a peg that the victim sat astride. The support for the feet, common in iconography, was unknown in antiquity. The victim was elevated little more than a foot or two above the ground and left to die of hunger and thirst. Death ensued in a few days and was sometimes hastened by the breaking of legs. It was a Jewish custom, not a Roman one, to give the condemned person a narcotic drink to lessen the pain. Crucifixion was a legal punishment until Constantine abolished it in the fourth century.

There are seven words from the cross. One of the seven is given by Mark and Matthew and by them alone; three are in Luke only; three are reported by John.

Mark and Matthew have Jesus cry out in desperation and abandonment: "My God, my God, why have you deserted me?" The fact that these are the opening words of Psalm 22 does not diminish the anguish of spirit which prompted them.

Luke adds words from the cross which reinforce the themes of his Gospel. The same Luke who alone gives us the key parables which expand forgiveness (good Samaritan and prodigal son) is the only evangelist to have Jesus pray: "Father, forgive them; they do not know what they are doing."

The same Jesus who gave life to the widow's son promises paradise to the dying thief. It is not only the grace Jesus bestows which startles but the unexpected recipients of it. Life is given to those who seem most bereft of it.

The same Luke who stressed the resignation of Jesus to his

destiny in Gethsemane stresses the trust of Jesus in God: "Father, into your hands I commit my spirit."

Luke alone had Mary accept God's plan in the annunciation: "I am the handmaid of the Lord . . . let what you have said be done to me." The son of Mary dies with similar words, words which are an annunciation of Easter, a herald, as they were for Mary, of new life.

Luke has Jesus die with the three most moving words from the cross. These words express forgiveness and mercy; they emphasize promise and trust. The dying Jesus, therefore, underscores the main themes of the Magnificat sung by his mother when life was young in her womb. In Luke, the crucified Jesus continues the parables and canticles which are typical of that Gospel.

Luke shows, throughout his Gospel, how people get second chances with God. This teaching is proclaimed from the cross as executioners and judges are forgiven, as a thief is reconciled, and even as Jesus himself will be granted a future by the Father into whose hands his spirit is committed.

As the lambs for Passover are slaughtered, Jesus is marked for death in John's Gospel. It is high noon when Pilate permits the execution. Mark observes that Jesus is before Pilate in the early morning and on the cross sometime before noon. In Mark's Gospel, there is darkness at noon and death in the afternoon. John gives a different chronology because of the symbolism.

Pilate announces "Behold the man!" and sends him to death about the time the lambs are killed. John began his Gospel with the Baptist announcing "Behold the lamb of God!"

Now, this symbolic lamb will be sacrificed in a ritual of memory and freedom. John carries this symbolism through by having the soldiers refrain from breaking the legs of Jesus on the cross. The Passover lamb was to have its blood shed but none of its bones broken.

In John's Gospel, Jesus controls his destiny, in the garden, before the high priest, in the dialogue with Pilate, and on the cross. All three Synoptics speak of a Simon of Cyrene who carries the cross of Jesus; John omits the reference but observes pointedly that Jesus went out of the city "carrying his own cross."

When Pilate gave up on Jesus, he said not only "Behold the man!" but "Here is your king." John's Gospel stresses the kingship of Jesus on the cross. It is only in John that the chief priests object strenuously to the inscription above the head of Jesus. To Pilate, they protest: "You should not write 'King of the Jews,' but 'This man said: I am King of the Jews.' " The inscription becomes a proclamation in the three crucial languages of religion, empire and culture (Hebrew, Latin and Greek). The Jesus on the cross is not a condemned insurrectionist but the lamb of God and the king of Israel. He is, furthermore, the high priest whose tunic is seamless. The Jewish historian Josephus tells us that the high priest wore a seamless tunic. Only John mentions this detail. Jesus dies, not abandoned and crying out in desolation as he does in Mark, but as the paschal Lamb who gives Israel Passover and freedom, as the king who is anointed and proclaimed, as the high priest who is consecrated and sacrificed.

John has Jesus declare three different words from the cross.

The first of these Johannine words calls attention to the women at the cross. All four evangelists record their presence. Mary Magdalene is the constant name in all the groupings. John alone mentions the mother of Jesus. Jesus addresses her with words that express not only the unbearable grief of Calvary but the transcendent joy of Christmas: "Woman, this is your son." The years from Christmas to Calvary were tragically few; the journey from manger to cross was completed with agonizing swiftness. The presence and the silence of Mary and the women intensify the anguish.

Women play an essential role in the life of Jesus; they are the most faithful of the disciples; they alone witness the entire life of Jesus, from birth to crucifixion, from Bethlehem, through Galilee, to Jerusalem. A woman holds Jesus in her arms on the first and last day of his life. Angels announce to women the birth of the Christ and the Easter return from death to life. Jesus is born and reborn as women witness, treasure these experiences in their hearts and announce them to the apostles.

In a second Johannine word from the cross, Jesus pleads "I am thirsty." John is careful to balance this physical need with a spiritual meaning. Jesus "knew that everything had now been completed and to fulfill the scripture perfectly" he speaks of his thirst. A sponge soaked with vinegar on a hyssop stick is raised to the crucified. Hyssop, fern-like, is less substantial than the reed mentioned by Mark and Matthew. Hyssop, however, is part of the Passover ritual cited in Exodus (12:22). Hyssop is used to sprinkle the blood of the paschal lamb on the doorposts of Israelite homes so that they may not be visited by the angel of death. The lamb dies so that the people may be set free.

"It is accomplished," Jesus now prays in the final Johannine word from the cross. Jesus is in sovereign control and determines when his death will occur. As he bows his head, he "gave up his spirit" to the world and the disciples. In John, Jesus, even on the cross, begins to live again.

And now a series of signs and wonders follows. The Synoptics tell us that the temple veil is violently torn from top to bottom. The temple is not now a building but the body of Jesus and the community of those who receive his spirit. The torn veil opens the temple to all. The first to enter the new temple are the Gentiles near the body of Jesus. They see through the veil. A Roman centurion confesses: "In truth, this man was a son of God."

Matthew is the only evangelist to tell us of the star which heralds the birth of Jesus. It is a gentle cosmic sign of light and glory. He is also the only evangelist who describes, in surrealistic terms, the cosmic disturbances as Jesus dies. The entire order of creation is shaken. There is darkness at noon in the skies above the earth, shattered rocks and tremors on the earth, open tombs and ghostly apparitions from beneath the earth.

The signs are different in John. They encircle the body of Jesus. The side of Jesus is pierced and blood and water come forth. The blood is a symbol of Passover and the Eucharist, the blood of the paschal lamb. The water is a symbol of the Spirit and baptism.

Jesus was born from Mary with the rush of blood and water that marks every birth. He dies as blood and water symbolize a new life for him. The new community is also born in blood and water from the body of Christ. There are signs of rebirth on every side as Jesus dies and is taken from the cross. The body of Jesus is the body of a king who has reigned from the cross and not been conquered by it; it is the body of a high priest who is not defiled by the cross but consecrates it.

Burial

The burial occurs at Calvary.

Matthew and John describe the incident most effectively.

In Matthew, we are told that another Joseph becomes the guardian of the deceased Jesus. This Joseph is not the carpenter from Nazareth but a prominent official from Arimathea. Pilate releases the body of the deceased Jesus, a counterpart of Herod who once sought the life of the child. Jesus is wrapped in clean linen; Luke told us of the infant in swaddling clothes. The tomb does not belong to Jesus; it is, like the manger, the property of a stranger.

In John, Jesus is buried in a garden, with one hundred pounds of myrrh and oils and spices. It is the burial of a king and a high priest. The garden reminds us of Eden and of Easter. We are on the verge of a new creation.

Conclusion

As we leave the hill of death, we are filled with memories of Gethsemane and the trials, of cross and tomb.

Three images of the crucified are especially indelible. The bowed head of the broken Jesus, overwhelmed with pain and death, is given by Mark and Matthew. The outstretched arms of the forgiving Jesus who prays for his executioners and commits himself into the hands of his Father is given by Luke. The inscription of kingship above the head of Jesus, the blood and water of priesthood, are given by John.

It has been a tragic night, the most tragic in the history of this world. The child of Christmas is gone, the star is not visible. The storyteller is silenced, the parables are heard no more. The table is empty, the bread consumed, the wine drained. There are no more words from the cross.

God is dead. Long live God.

V

A Eulogy at the Tomb

Why is it that we feel that we have just buried, not a man, but life itself? Perhaps everyone who buries a life companion feels the same. Questions about the worth of going on are spontaneous and incessant at such a time.

And now, there are only memories. The memories are not in the tomb but in our hearts. All that we take with us as we leave this place are the memories. The presence is gone; the body is not visible; the words are finished. Such finality! Such absence!

He once told us a story about a prodigal son whose memory of his father's love brought him back home. Memories renew life when all the other resources are exhausted. No one can take our memories from us. Perhaps the best gifts we give one another are the memories.

No grave can hold our memories of Jesus. It seems to be the only part of him we have not entombed.

There is darkness all around us today. There is no sun, no moonlight, no stars. We feel the spring air on Calvary but no flowers are visible and the colors of the rainbow have faded from sight.

Memory is a blessing but also a wound. Memories are like

thorns which create new injuries even though they protect the flower. Memories mean the pain of this loss will never go away.

And yet if the memory dies, all hope goes with it. We learn today that hope is fashioned from suffering. We pay a price for our memories.

When he washed our feet, more was demanded of him than we knew. Now, we know. We know because we feel the pain as we bring the memory back.

How shall we remember him? As someone who believed in us—too much for his own welfare. We were not as reliable as he believed. His love frightened us, the way light startles darkness and spring unsettles winter, the way rain takes the desert by surprise. Life sometimes recoils from the very need it has to continue. Today is one of those times. Love makes its certitude out of ambiguities.

He is gone and he seems to have taken his faith in us with him. We feel like a widow who lost her only son, like a father whose child left him for a distant country. We are bereft, abandoned.

But the memory persists. And so we shall seek him, if need be, through the centuries in bread and wine. We shall repeat his words so that hearing them again we may sense his nearness. It is the only way we have to bring him back from the dead, to call him from a distant country.

We seek him now in one another. But there is not enough of him in any one of us. It is only when we assemble as a community that we meet him in the way we require. Together we shall be faithful to his belief in our goodness. Even though we are unworthy we shall trust in his faith to make us better.

Today, it is not out of place to remember Christmas even here on Calvary. Does not every mother recall the birth of her child at graveside? It is fitting.

Here, by the empty cross and the sealed tomb, the star of his birth is not visible. Bethlehem seems so far away that we have no hope of reaching it. The gold and frankincense are gone—the myrrh remains. Myrrh is not only a gift for the child but an oil for burial. Joseph is dead and Mary, the widow, keeps vigil. The woman of the annunciation and the Magnificat becomes today the mother of sorrows and Pietà.

The good Samaritan is buried, crucified by those he healed on the road. The father of the prodigal son has been nailed to the cross with his arms outstretched, forgiving. We heard those impossible words "Father, forgive . . ." just hours ago. The father welcomed back the lost son with tears of joy and gestures of love. He never forgot his son. There is such joy when you hold a memory in your arms. Now, the tears are tears of pain and absence, tears of Rachel weeping for her children because they are no more.

He came among his own and we received him not . . . to the inn and there was no room. The manger is empty. There is no one to wash his feet. It is no longer possible to share bread and wine with him.

Mary's body once gave forth blood and water as Jesus was born. On the cross, blood and water came from his side. The son gave birth to the mother who gave him life. The community of those who remember him was born.

With no reason to justify the hope, we believe, even in this darkness, that the star will shine again and that there will always be magi to follow it. Why is despair the better course?

69

We believe that we shall find the right road to Bethlehem and that the child will live again and receive our gifts.

We shall find our way to the garden where the tree of life flourishes and this time we shall be allowed to eat of it. And there we shall meet the storyteller once more. The spring air and the sunlight will reveal the flowers and God's promise will cross the sky with rainbows.

We shall never lose Christ. If we do not follow him, he will follow us . . . not too closely lest he take away our freedom . . . but near enough to wash our feet when we are ready . . . close enough to give us bread and wine in our weariness. He will love us whenever we choose. We know this, not from reason but from memories.

Jesus lives again in every child, in every star, in every rainbow, in every Samaritan, in every father seeking a lost son, in every mother at the cross. The best gift Jesus gave was the very memory of him left in our hearts as death took him away.

VI

Advent Watch

It is easier to begin once than to start all over again. Beginnings seem to be made for first times and not for second starts.

How do we begin now that it is finished? It is painful to know in advance that the best is gone, that even a successful second effort will fail to equal all that once was. Life is easier when initial attempts stay the course. The exhaustion of a dream makes further dreams unappealing.

How does memory get beyond the tomb? When people are alive, we are never quite sure about where they are. Once we bury them, there is only one place to find them. Total predictability is the same as death. To be in only one place forever is to be lost.

The most frightening thing about the tomb is the fact that it ends all change. The living change and the dead are part of that no more.

The tomb is the last word spoken, the final image. The voice of Jesus is silent. He is seen no more.

Yet, in some ways, there is mercy in the tomb. At least, the pain is finished. The horror of the cross is gone. The nails have been removed.

The thud of his body against the wood . . . the efficiency of the soldiers . . . the fact that life went on in the city . . . that one could hear the merchants and the children, as though nothing of consequence was happening on the cross . . . the sound of the lance as it broke through his flesh . . . that it was all done in the sight of his mother.

The tomb is better. We offer the dead the mercy we deny the living.

There is mercy in the tomb. At last there is a place for him. In his birth, there was no room for him. In his life, he had nowhere to lay his head. The cross was no place for a human being. The tomb is better. That such a place is better!

Why are we more merciful with the dead? Is it because they are no longer free? When people stay in one place, when they change no more, they are easy to control.

Is the tomb our way of saying we prefer a Jesus we can control?

Do some Christians want the Church to be a tomb? Always in one place . . . predictable . . . a community of those forever docile, controllable, enclosed. When the Church is a tomb, it is ordered and well kept. Cemeteries are seldom messy, often extravagantly manicured; they are not difficult to keep neat. But tombs lack all the exuberance of life, all its unpredictability, all its failure and mistakes, all its disorder.

Does the Church at times become merciful with its dead members? Considerate only with those who never grow, make no demands, resist change, avoid mistakes, stay in place?

Is this what Jesus came to teach us?

The rubrics and rituals of the execution of Jesus were exact; the liturgy of the way we killed him, meticulous.

His birth was not like that. The turbulence and turmoil of birth . . . the exuberance of an utterly unpredictable new life. The manger was not a tomb and so the child left it easily.

There are no rubrics for bringing about birth . . . the rubrics of execution are more impressive. But who wants such a liturgy, such a ritual, such a rubric of despair? In the tomb, there is no turbulence.

The parables followed no rubrics. They were vivid stories, told by a young man who loved life so much it seemed he would never die. The stories were so filled with life that they never died in us. We would not become the tomb for dead stories. We would tell the stories with unpredictable consequences for ourselves and for others.

They were dangerous stories, stories no institution could feel comfortable with, stories that made community happen, stories that evaded the tomb of our dead selves and our dead institutions.

There are no rituals for good stories; they are different everytime we hear them. The language of doctrine is rigid and precise; the language of stories is resilient and pliable. We memorize creeds, not parables. How many times have we heard about the Samaritan and the prodigal son? They are different every time. We find ourselves in the stories; there is a less significant place for us in the creeds. Institutions prefer creeds to stories, professions of loyalty and fidelity to wonder and creativity. It is not that institutions and creeds are dispensable or unimportant. Institutions and creeds define the parameters.

They secure life rather than make it happen. They limit rather than encourage risk.

How many times have we heard the parable of the life of Jesus? There always seems to be a place for us in it. We are there, somewhere, in the birth and the Last Supper, the bread and the wine, the washing of the feet and the farewell discourse, the betrayal and Gethsemane, the trials and the cross, the dying and the burial.

This week we long for the story again. It seems as though we hear it for the first time. The parable of the life of Jesus enchants and renews us. The pain touches us but so does the elegance and the glory. The human spirit of Jesus prevails and we all become the victors.

And yet, today, he is in the tomb. That fact seems as immovable and unavoidable as the huge stone across the entrance.

There is mercy in the tomb. At least we don't hear the hammer and the nails. And yet this is not entirely true. They shall echo in our memories for as long as we live. But at least we know the nails are out of his flesh, even though the life has gone out of his body as well.

There is mercy in the tomb. At least we don't hear that awful cry of abandonment from the cross. "My God, my God, why have you deserted me?" The cry makes us fear that his spirit as well as his body will be destroyed.

The tomb is better than that. He has at last a place in this world. We finally found an inn that had room for him. We were the good Samaritans who carried him from the cross last night and found an inn, off the open road.

Everything died last night, even our hope. Somewhere in

the tomb Jesus is buried and, with him, our future. Who wants hope in such a world anyway?

We began with memories of Christmas. And now the child is in the tomb. Everything in us rebels against the death of a child. A child is made for the disorder of life, not for the order of death. The community of Christ is to be a gathering of children, not a congregation of guardians. Love has none of the efficiency of law. A child is too filled with life for rubrics and rules, for rituals of despair and liturgies of burial. The Christmas hope that the child Jesus embodied must not be crushed by the stone across the tomb. It must not end with the hands of the child nailed, the child's heart broken by the lance. Somehow a star must be visible from the tomb.

And yet we know the tomb is unconquerable. It is all over. Hope is only fantasy.

Even if we could bring Jesus back, would it be right? Why would we bring him back? For us? We are not worthy of his return.

What do we make of all this?

Even the Church does not know what to do with Holy Saturday. It is the only day of the year that has no liturgy of its own.

We can do nothing for Jesus in the tomb. It makes no sense to wash his feet; we cannot come to him for bread or to share wine; he tells no stories now. And even if we leave gifts at the tomb, there is no one to receive them.

All we can do at the tomb is remember and wait. We are lost between Passover memories and Advent expectations. We need Easter to change both into the bread and wine of life.

The time has come for waiting. But all waiting has something to do with hope. Is this why we wait at the tomb? We have hope . . . even for the dead Jesus.

Even on the brink of despair, we know that there was only so much of Jesus they could kill or bury. Somehow Jesus was in the stars and the sunshine, in the bread and the wine, in the words and the memories. They could not darken the stars and the sunshine, take away wheat and wine, make everyone forget the words, erase all the memories. Part of him is in the tomb; part of him is in the fabric of life, in the flesh of human existence.

Here, at the tomb, we wait, for all of Christ to return. It is an impossible hope. Life does not come from the tomb, no more than a virgin gives birth to a child. But the season is spring. Everything in spring tells us the tomb of winter is open, the stone of death has been removed, and life is possible everywhere.

Easter Morning

It is dawn, a faint light, first day. There are, of course, no magi. That was a long time ago. Now there are three women, bearing gifts of spices and oil. They follow the star also, the daystar of Easter Sunday morning.

It is an impossible journey, like that of the magi. But the magi sought and found. The women have diminished expectations. They seek, not life, but someone strong enough to open the tomb.

Jesus once told us that if we asked for bread he would not give us a stone.

But the stone of death is so final, so immovable. Surely, we

77

cannot find the bread of life there. All the wine of his life is gone; the alleluia days have run their course.

And yet, as long as dawn resists the darkness, as long as a star shines, how could we not take impossible journeys?

What makes us set forth is this strange notion, this wild poetry that tells us some lives are never over, that some lives are too disorderly for burial.

Jesus is for birth rather than for burial. Birth is disorderly; no one stays still to be born.

There are always magi when a star is in the sky.

But these magi of the dawn are women, the very opposite of the symbols of power that put Jesus in the tomb. Perhaps it is fitting that the new magi be women. No woman condemned Jesus. Annas and Caiaphas, Herod and Pilate, Judas and Peter, soldiers and executioners were, of course, men.

The star once led to Bethlehem but the Christmas story, we observed, was depicted with the shadows of Calvary and the light of Easter. There was death and survival in the story, departure and return.

The star once led to Bethlehem but it was a journey, we reminded ourselves, one had to take all the way. It is wrong to seek only the manger, only the cross, only the tomb, only Easter. The journey is misdirected until all the points en route are properly traversed. Each element in the story is colored by other elements. An abridged version destroys the parable and the meaning.

The angel of annunciation once told a woman the impossible story of virginity and conception. And she believed. Indeed, her faith allowed the story to happen. It was not incidental to the process.

The women magi encounter another angel of annunciation, an Easter angel, who tells them the impossible story of a dead man, the only son of his mother, a widow, who has survived all the horror of the cross and who now lives again. And they believe, with a faith not incidental to the Easter event.

In the garden, on Easter morning, by Calvary, the women magi tell us that not a bone of his body is broken, that the paschal lamb is whole and entire, the wounds have healed, the stone is gone, the tomb is empty and Christ has become bread for the world. He who was crushed on the Mount of Olives has returned to anoint us; he whose very life was pressed from his body offers us the wine of immortality. We have been given a high priest, not subject to death, a king of glory, not subject to defeat.

The women magi tell us that all the promise of Christ's life is intact and that the storyteller has returned without the nails, with his faith in us undiminished, with an even greater story to tell us. The manger and the tomb are empty and our hearts are full.

The Gospels do not describe Easter. They announce it. The Gospels did not describe the crucifixion nor the virginal conception. These events are announced. Genesis did not describe creation. It announced it.

And so we are expected to announce Easter to one another, not to explain it nor defend it. When we see a star, we do not describe it, we announce it. Each of us must do his or her own seeing.

Jesus is not dead. Do the dead have that much life through the centuries? The bread of life, the wine of love are inexhaustible.

There is no harmony or order in the Easter accounts as there is in the crucifixion story. Of all the stories about Jesus, the most disorderly are those of Christmas and Easter.

The Christmas event is strikingly different, as we know, in Matthew and in Luke. All four evangelists speak of Easter. Yet, on only two points are they in agreement: the tomb is empty on Sunday morning; Mary Magdalene (the only constant name in all accounts) and other women disciples discover the empty tomb.

The Christmas accounts agreed on only two points: the birth occurs in Bethlehem; Mary, the mother, conceives as a virgin and Joseph is her husband.

Women initiate the Christmas and the Easter stories.

The Gospel accounts speak about how difficult it was to recognize the risen Christ. The difficulty may have been due to a desire to see Jesus as he was, in the past. In later history, disciples will also resist the new forms Christ takes or the Church assumes.

Since the early disciples had not yet made the whole journey with Christ, they do not recognize him. It is Easter but the disciples are still with the parables or Calvary, focused on the cross or the tomb. They have not yet made it into the future.

The Easter Christ is not memory but future. The Easter Christ goes before us, into Galilee, ascending into heaven, sending the Spirit.

Christ does not lead us back to Bethlehem. He makes no nostalgic returns to the cross; he does not take us to the tomb to see the stones and the linens and the emptiness.

Where do we find him now that the cross has flowered into the empty tomb, now that the tomb has become Easter's manger?

We find him in what he loved most, namely in one another. We find him most especially when bread is broken in friendship.

Jesus comes out of the tomb for us. It is only Easter when Jesus appears in our gatherings.

Easter is to be the foundation of our community life. It is the event meant to be present in all our relationships.

John's Gospel is especially striking. Christ returns to assure us of two gifts: peace and forgiveness.

Peace and forgiveness are the final gifts of the Christ Child to us; they are present in those who have received with a faithful heart the bread and the wine of Passover, the cleansing in water and the covenant memory of the Last Supper.

It is Christmas time in Galilee, not only in Judea where Jesus is born but in Galilee where he goes before us in Easter glory.

And now the impossible journey is complete. We have gone all the way from Christmas to Easter. And we find that the end is like the beginning, although now we see it for the first time. Christmas is different after Easter.

The wonder of this journey is that it never ends. It is a circle.

Just as a child asks us to do it again whenever we do something mystical, playful, exciting, magical, joyful, so we ask to do the journey again. A child never wants happiness only once.

And so, for as long as we live, we shall do it again, from Christmas to Easter. And each time it will be as though it had never been done.

It is wonderful to know that after the dawn of Easter, the Bethlehem star will shine again. Mary of Nazareth will outlive Herod the Great and even Pilate.

It is wonderful to know that as the journey goes on we shall meet the magi and see their gifts, hear angelic music and shepherd song.

It is wonderful to know the widow's tears turn to joy and that the Father's arms are always open.

It is wonderful to know that the Last Supper becomes the first Eucharist and that the farewell discourse is about never going away.

It is wonderful to know that the Samaritan finds us and that Peter is forgiven.

It is wonderful to know that the tomb is empty and our hearts are full.

It is wonderful to know that the three women magi announce Easter and that all our doubts are changed into the bread and wine of faith.

It is wonderful to know that as we do this journey again we shall find the Easter Child in the manger and that the Christmas Child will be born from the blood and water of the cross.

It is wonderful to know that *we* are now the manger and to know that the community the risen Christ returns to is ourselves.

It is wonderful to know that because Christ is risen, you and I are the resurrection and the life.

VII

Sunday Sunrise

We shall never lose hope, not after having shared in the events from Christmas to Calvary. Hope comes from memories, experiences, grace and vision. We have lived through a three-day retreat in which hope has prevailed against overwhelming negativity.

And now, even as we speak, the darkness is dispelled and the glory of an Easter sunrise announces the good news that Christ is risen. He has banished the shadows of death, broken the bonds of the grave and sheds light on all the world.

The morning sun, new-born like a Christmas child, is an Easter angel bathing us in sunlight as death releases its dark grip. The spring air unwraps the burial linens of winter and life comes forth.

Luke tells a long and beautiful story about two disciples at Emmaus who spend Easter afternoon and evening with Jesus. They recognize him the way we recognize him, in hearing what the Scriptures proclaim and in the breaking of the bread. We are an Emmaus community this morning watching the sun rise, sensing Christ at our side as the Scriptures are opened and the bread is blessed.

In John's Gospel, we are at the tomb earlier in the day. It

is to Mary Magdalene that the risen Christ speaks before he speaks to anyone else. Like the disciples at Emmaus, she does not recognize Christ immediately but only after some words and some time with him.

Christ greets Mary the way the father of the prodigal son must have greeted him, by saying the name in joy. Jesus restores her with a word. Genesis describes creation as the result of God's creative word. Here, by the tomb, life is created again as Christ says a word.

Christ looks at Mary. He had looked at Peter two days before, during the trial. This look is filled with joy and peace. He says "Mary" and we all know that the Lord has returned and has brought his faith in us with him.

The Gospel stories have come full circle. Christmas began as the angel said: "Mary." Another woman, Elizabeth, recognized Jesus not yet in the breaking of bread but in the womb of Mary. It is at this moment that Mary sings her Magnificat, already an Easter song as she herself prepares for Christmas. Women recognize Jesus in the darkness of the womb and in the shadows of the tomb. They are the first to perceive the light of Christmas and the glory of Easter.

Mary Magdalene is at the feet of Christ as an earlier Mary was in the Martha-Mary story. These three women named Mary are the magi who journey toward the light of a new discipleship. Mary of Nazareth gives us the flesh and blood of Jesus; Mary, the sister of Martha, gives birth to Christ by attentiveness to his word; Mary Magdalene is the first to welcome the risen Christ with Easter faith.

It is a joyous day.

We shall never lose hope, not after all of this. Jesus told us

in the Passover farewell that he would not leave us orphans or friendless. He has been true to his word. This day, more than all others, there are no widows or orphans or strangers.

We have passed over into new life even as night has passed into dawn.

It is finished now, not life or even the journey but merely this celebration of this phase of it. We have done all this in memory of him.

And now it is time to go. It is time to leave the empty tomb and even to go beyond Emmaus. We shall do the journey again. We must.

For already the Easter sun announcing the risen Christ is a magi star promising the Christmas Child. The sun is a star. You and I have seen it. O holy night! O happy day!

And so we shall go from Jerusalem this morning back to Bethlehem. And we shall meet Christ there. For, now, Christ is everywhere.